BELUGA WHALES

by **Elizabeth R. Johnson**

Consultant:
Jody Rake, Member,
Southwest Marine Educators Association

CAPSTONE PRESS
a capstone imprint

Pebble Plus is published by Capstone Press,
1710 Roe Crest Drive, North Mankato, Minnesota 56003
www.mycapstone.com

Library of Congress Cataloging-in-Publication Data
Names: Johnson, Elizabeth R., 1986–author.
Title: Beluga whales / by Elizabeth R. Johnson.
Description: North Mankato, Minnesota : Capstone Press, [2017] | Series:
  Pebble plus. Sea life | Audience: Ages 4–8. | Audience: K to grade 3. |
  Includes bibliographical references and index.
Identifiers: LCCN 2015049116 | ISBN 9781515720812 (library binding) | ISBN
  9781515720850 (eBook PDF)
Subjects: LCSH: White whale—Juvenile literature.
Classification: LCC QL737.C433 J625 2017 | DDC 599.5/42—dc23
LC record available at http://lccn.loc.gov/2015049116

Editorial Credits
Jaclyn Jaycox, editor; Philippa Jenkins, designer;
Svetlana Zhurkin, media researcher; Gene Bentdahl, production specialist

Photo Credits
Alamy: Peter Steiner, 11; National Geographic Creative: Norbert Rosing, 15; Newscom: ZUMA Press/Andrey Nekrasov, 13, 17; Shutterstock: Buchan, 19, Christopher Meder, 9, Luna Vandoorne, 5, Miles Away Photography, 21, Ralf Juergen Kraft, back cover, 3, 6, 14, 23, 24, Sparkling Moments Photography, 7; SuperStock: Biosphoto, cover

Design Elements by Shutterstock

Note to Parents and Teachers

The Sea Life set supports national science standards related to life science. This book describes and illustrates beluga whales. The images support early readers in understanding the text. The repetition of words and phrases helps early readers learn new words. This book also introduces early readers to subject-specific vocabulary words, which are defined in the Glossary section. Early readers may need assistance to read some words and to use the Table of Contents, Glossary, Read More, Internet Sites, and Index sections of the book.

Printed in China.
022016   007718

Table of Contents

The White Whales

Beluga whales are easy to spot in the ocean. They have white skin and a big round forehead called a melon. Like all whales, belugas are mammals.

Belugas are small whales.
They are about 15 feet
(4.6 meters) long. Belugas
can weigh as much as
3,000 pounds (1,360 kilograms).

Up Close

Belugas can hear and see
well in water. To swim, they
move their flukes. They can
swim forward and backward.
Pectoral fins help them steer.

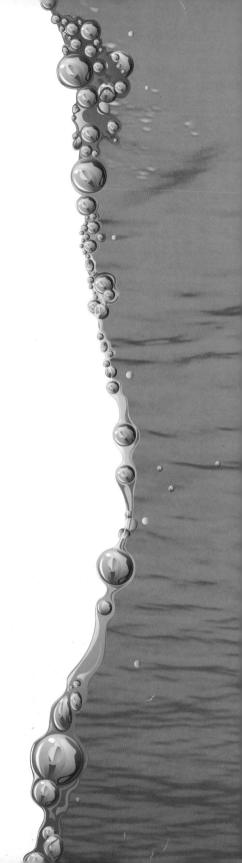

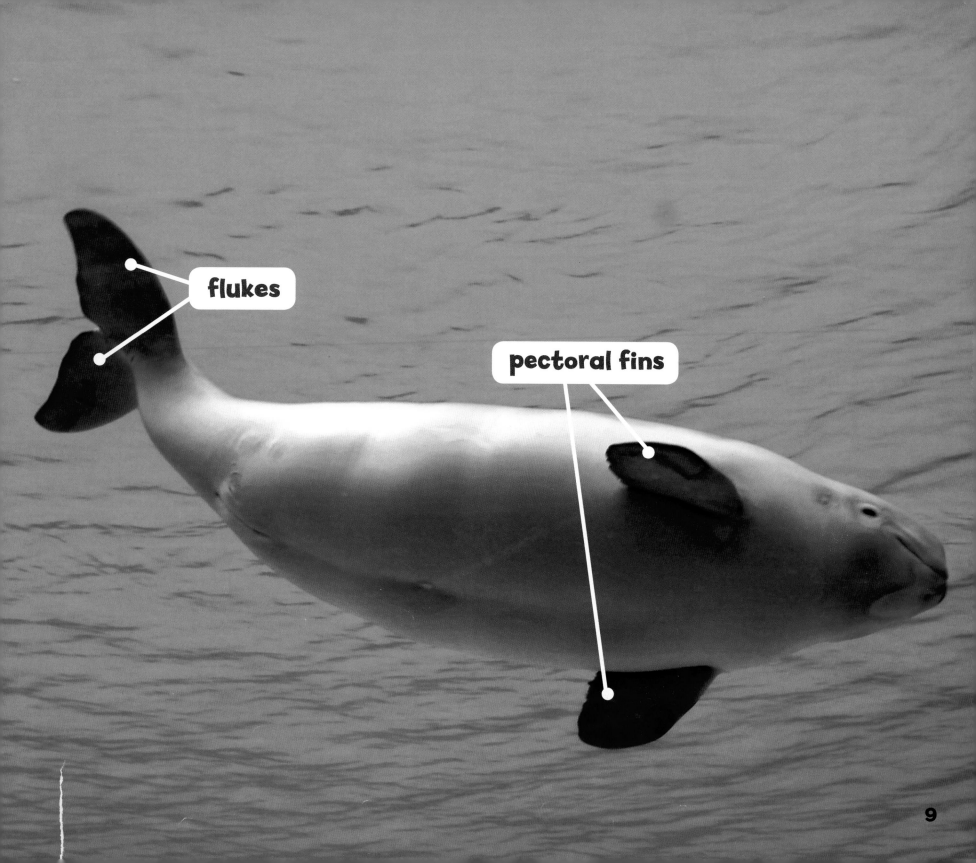

flukes

pectoral fins

Belugas often swim in shallow water. But they dive as deep as 2,123 feet (647 m)! Belugas rise to the surface to breathe. Their blowholes open to take in air.

Where Do Belugas Live?

Belugas live in the Arctic Ocean.

The water there is very cold.

Thick layers of blubber keep

belugas warm.

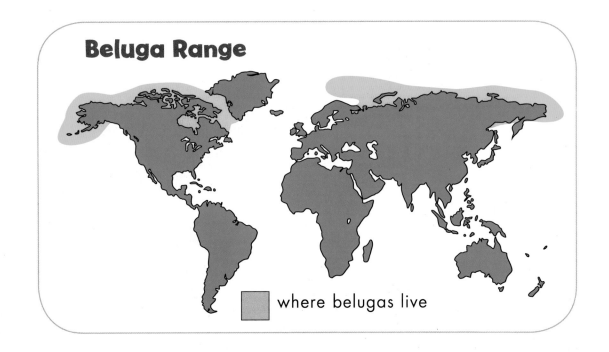

Beluga Range

where belugas live

When the Arctic Ocean freezes, belugas migrate south. They live and travel in pods. A pod can have a few whales or hundreds.

Life as a Beluga

Belugas use sounds and echoes to find prey. This process is called echolocation. Belugas eat octopuses, squid, crabs, snails, and fish.

Belugas love to make noise!
They communicate in clicks,
whistles, and clangs. They can
even copy human sounds.

Baby belugas are called calves.
They are born gray or brown.
Calves turn white when they
are 6 or 7 years old. Belugas
live for 30 to 35 years.

Glossary

blowhole—a hole on the top of a whale's head; whales breathe air through blowholes

blubber—a thick layer of fat under the skin of some animals; blubber keeps animals warm

echolocation—the process of using sounds and echoes to locate objects; whales and dolphins use echolocation to find food

fluke—the wide, flat area at the end of a whale's tail; whales move their flukes to swim

mammal—a warm-blooded animal that breathes air; mammals have hair or fur; female mammals feed milk to their young

migrate—to move from one place to another

pectoral fins—a pair of fins found on each side of the head

pod—a group of whales; beluga pods range from less than five whales to several hundred whales

prey—an animal hunted by another animal for food

shallow—not deep

surface—the outside or outermost layer of something

Read More

Beaton, Kathryn. *Discover Beluga Whales.* Splash! Ann Arbor, Michigan: Cherry Lake Publishing, 2016.

Meister, Cari. *Totally Wacky Facts About Sea Animals.* Mind Benders. North Mankato, Minn.: Capstone Press, 2016.

Riggs, Kate. *Whales.* Seedlings. Mankato, Minn.: Creative Education, 2015.

Internet Sites

FactHound offers a safe, fun way to find Internet sites related to this book. All of the sites on FactHound have been researched by our staff.

Here's all you do:

Visit *www.facthound.com*

Type in this code: 9781515720812

 Check out projects, games and lots more at **www.capstonekids.com**

Index